———CONT'

C000183372

Poetry Book Society

CHOICE SELECTORS RECOMMENDATION SPECIAL COMMENDATION	SARAH HOWE & ANTHONY ANAXAGOROU
TRANSLATION SELECTOR	HARRY JOSEPHINE GILES
PAMPHLET SELECTORS	NINA MINGYA POWLES & NICK MAKOHA
CONTRIBUTORS	SOPHIE O'NEILL NATHANIEL SPAIN KYM DEYN LEDBURY CRITICS
EDITORIAL & DESIGN	ALICE KATE MULLEN

Poetry Book Society Memberships
Choice
4 Books a Year: 4 Choice books & 4 *Bulletins* (UK £55, Europe £65, ROW £75)
World
8 Books: 4 Choices, 4 Translation books & 4 *Bulletins* (£98, £120, £132)
Complete
24 Books: 4 Choices, 16 Recommendations, 4 Translations & 4 *Bulletins* (£223, £265, £292)

Single copies of the *Bulletin* £9.99

Cover Art Nestan Abdushelishvili, *Tkibuli* (ტყიბული) *Kids*, 2018
Copyright Poetry Book Society and contributors. All rights reserved.
ISBN 9781913129408 ISSN 0551-1690

Poetry Book Society | Milburn House | Dean Street | Newcastle upon Tyne | NE1 1LF
0191 230 8100 | enquiries@poetrybooksociety.co.uk
WWW.POETRYBOOKS.CO.UK

LETTER FROM THE PBS

As this *Bulletin* arrives with you, we will have just finished our major poetry event of the year, the Newcastle Poetry Festival which took place at the beginning of May. We are so excited to have been part of a live event once again and we really hope that those of you who could attend in person found it as positive an experience as we did. We'll be returning to Coventry in July at the Skylines Festival of Poetry and Spoken Word, so Midlands members (and others), we look forward to seeing you there!

We have a remarkable selection of titles to take you through the summer – I really hope you find *Emblem*, this season's Choice from Lucy Mercer, as fascinating and thought-provoking as we have. We hope you are inspired by the varied PBS Recommendations too, all of which offer new ways of thinking and seeing and combine to make really profound and stimulating reads. And thanks to Holly Hopkins for the aptly titled *The English Summer*, our summer Special Commendation.

With these selections, it's time to say a huge thank you and fond farewell to Sarah Howe, this *Bulletin* contains her final selections for the PBS. She will be replaced by Mona Arshi whose selections and commentary we will welcome in the Autumn *Bulletin*.

Thanks so much to those of you who completed our recent PBS member survey. We really appreciate you taking the time to share your thoughts on your membership and our work. We will be using all your feedback to help shape the short and long-term plans for the PBS which we will share with you in due course!

SOPHIE O'NEILL
PBS & INPRESS DIRECTOR

LUCY MERCER

Lucy Mercer's poems have been published widely in magazines such as *Poetry London*, *Poetry Review* and *The White Review*, and in anthologies like *Altered States* (Ignota, 2022). She was awarded the inaugural White Review Poet's Prize. She has collaborated with artists to produce work for Glasgow International and Kunstverein Freiburg, as well as a text-image pamphlet *Renewal* (Kelder Press, 2021). Her first collection *Emblem* reuses images from Andrea Alciato's early modern emblem book the *Emblematum liber*. She recently completed a PhD in which she developed a speculative theory of emblems, and teaches creative writing at Goldsmiths.

EMBLEM

PROTOTYPE | £12.00 | PBS PRICE £9.00

In *Emblem*, Lucy Mercer reaches back into history to commune with the emblem book, an obscure Renaissance genre which combined riddling illustrations with verses drawing out their lessons about how readers should live. Mercer's *Emblem* is less interested in stable moral meanings, however, than in moments of uncertainty and unsettled perception, as repeatedly figured by the optical trickery of mirrors or "water distorting in a bucket". Still, the book is infused with some of the strangeness of that lost world: its belief in hermetic symbols, their proximity to magic.

Only in the book's final section, 'Emblemata', does Mercer reproduce a series of original woodcut prints and add her own poems, though one doesn't straightforwardly illustrate the other. Instead, there are flashes of relation, as she breathes new life into the centuries-old woodcuts. A title, 'Obscurity', sits above an ornate print of a twining plant; below, a quatrain offers a kind of *ars poetica*:

> Poetry: she moves like ivy
> every word re-encoding itself...

There is a Rorschach quality to these poems. Freud was not the first to point out that the language of dreams resembles that of images or hieroglyphics. Mercer follows the nudges of the unconscious wherever they lead, to thrilling effect:

> Past a spilled person resting in wet lines,
> soldiers lacing swords over me, a tree.
> Here I am sightless & you voiceless?
> Tell me again, tell me again in the dark.

This historical frame is placed around very contemporary concerns: certain themes and preoccupations recur, including the relation between soul and body, image and text, voice and silence, mother and child. Particularly vivid is the enclosed domesticity of solo motherhood, whose lonely early days re-echo across the collection in a sort of fantasia:

> my twin daughters
> when they were born
> felt light as sprains in both arms

SARAH HOWE

LUCY MERCER

Emblems are a hybrid form of text and image, that were printed using woodcuts during the early modern period. I began writing *Emblem* when I was pregnant with my son. At that time, I had also begun to study Andrea Alciato's emblem book, *Emblematum Liber* (1531), and the book is a result of that strange admixture. I began to wonder if thinking how text and image relate to each other might be a substitute for thinking about how a mother relates to a child, or a body to a mind, or past to present, or how in motherhood not only do children appear, but many other selves as well. I thought a lot of Annie Dillard writing about seeing an excavation of clay figures: "Seeing the broad earth under the open sky, and a patch of it sliced in deep corridors from which bodies emerge, surprises many people to tears."

Like motherhood and poetry, I can't say that I understand emblems any more than I did when I started reading them – I have been more drawn to their physical, changing materiality, and the way they provide a structure or frame for composting or processing things: a dialogue. But, a dialogue with what can't be understood (it has been helpful that I can't actually read Latin). This not-knowing was in general what guided the poems: it seemed to me that there was a shared quality of obscurity pervading both emblems and motherhood, an obscurity that is also in my mind associated with poetic logic and perhaps is foundational to being. In the grey hours of early motherhood one also finds oneself in this liminal space. I would hope that *Emblem* is not a confessional memoir, but more of a drifting in and out of that place – which Henry Corbin called the *mundus imaginalis*, and a world of images where perhaps, things are neither living nor dead.

LUCY RECOMMENDS

Emily Berry, *Unexhausted Time* (Faber); Sam Buchan-Watts, *Path Through Wood* (Prototype); Thomas Campion, *Ayres & Observations* (Carcanet); Eve Esfandiari Denney, *My Bodies This Morning This Evening* (Bad Betty Press); Peter Gizzi, *Sky Burial* (Carcanet); Louise Glück, *Faithful and Virtuous Night* (Carcanet); Daisy Lafarge, *Life Without Air* (Granta); Lila Matsumoto, *Two Twin Pipes Sprout Water* (Prototype); Carl Phillips, *Pale Colors in a Tall Field* (Farrar, Straus and Giroux); Mary Ruefle, *Dunce* (Wave Books); Kandace Siobhan Walker, *Kaleido* (Bad Betty Press).

I CHOICE

IMAGO

I walk up to a black bucket
full of water and full of an image,
it's a reflection again

if I could see above, it would not
startle me.

we are in an invisible harness,
Andrea,
but it's only with asymmetries

like water distorting in a bucket
like the shock of being entered by another
like a birthday that was easier last year –
that we can believe we are moving.

this is the beloved who walks around and closes
the eyes of carnations in the air.

ICARUS

I've come to see someone about a thing.
Its surface is separated in waves like the ribs
of wild boar roasted by the fires of men.

This thing is suspended and silent.
The unnoticed garden, the kitchen blind lit peach
with indoorsness this mid-afternoon in winter

Like a pair of lungs that had been flying
towards the outside coughing hard and dry,
a child's cough. But then had stopped.

Inhale, it would say, if it had a voice.
Just inhale the air as if you are also a fire.

VICTORIA ADUKWEI BULLEY

Victoria Adukwei Bulley is a poet, writer and artist. An alumna of the Barbican Young Poets and recipient of an Eric Gregory Award, Victoria has held residencies in the US, Brazil and the V&A Museum in London. Her debut pamphlet, *Girl B*, was published by the African Poetry Book Fund in 2017. She is the recipient of a Techne scholarship for doctoral research at Royal Holloway, University of London.

QUIET

FABER | £10.99 | PBS PRICE £8.25

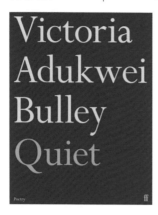

Victoria Adukwei Bulley's *Quiet* is extraordinary for many reasons, not least the depth of its combined poetic and conceptual enquiry into anti-blackness, present and historical. An epigraph from the theorist Kevin Quashie points us towards a more nuanced picture of black culture than the headline focus on resistance might allow: "It is this exploration, this reach toward the inner life, that an aesthetic of quiet makes possible; and it is this that is the path to a sweet freedom". One poem teases out the many overlapping senses of "quiet":

> as in slow to anger /
> as in shy /
> as in sulking or sullen /
> as in nice /
> as in clean, tree-lined streets /
> as in well-resourced libraries /

A, yes, quietly telling tour-de-force, this series of glosses slowly reveals the racialised, gendered and class-based lines along which that word's customary usages fall.

Several other poems make innovative use of listing as a structural device. There's the invocation-as-incantation of 'ode' – "oh my diablo, diablo pequeno, oh night singer" – whose headlong rush lies somewhere between exuberance and desperate prayer. Or there is the first section of, "revision", which tells its story of colonial plunder via a series of "delete as appropriate" options:

> from the 1400s, the area later known as *the gold coast* would be (choose one)
> *discovered / invaded / visited / landed upon*

It's a form that brings with it a sense of empire's bureaucratic banality, while raising the question of individual responsibility (that misleading instruction – "choose one") in reckoning with such histories. Bulley's poems are clear-eyed in their commitments, while glinting with irony:

> ...worry not. the [white]
> supremacist capitalist [insert -ist] [insert -ist] patriarchy is working faultlessly
> today, running at full service; no disruptions, even with your small axe in its back

Brilliant, they cut to the quick.

    SARAH HOWE

I SELECTOR'S COMMENT

VICTORIA ADUKWEI BULLEY

"She had an inside and an outside now and suddenly she knew how not to mix them." – Zora Neale Hurston, *Their Eyes Were Watching God*

"The idea of quiet, then, can shift attention to what is interior."
– Kevin Quashie, *The Sovereignty of Quiet: Beyond Resistance in Black Culture*

When I first set out to put *Quiet* together I wasn't sure that the ideas I was exploring would be coherent, let alone interesting to anyone beyond myself. I worried that the poems were, ironically, too quiet – that it would be difficult to sustain writing around a concept that might just as easily be described as a mood or feeling. I was trying to articulate something both real and also difficult to grasp – about black introversion, for one, but also about the particular structural imperative placed upon the black subject to perennially give testimony to racialised suffering – as a way of validating, alleviating (and reproducing) that suffering – at the same time as the demand to be silent, well-mannered; unseen. I wanted to paint something of that psychic tension, and it wasn't until I was introduced to the work of Kevin Quashie, quoted above, that the way forward – or rather, inward – crystalised.

Like the interior, *Quiet* does not pretend to offer maps. It resists the giving of directions or advice. It is less of a manifesto, and more of a meditation. And yet, too, like the interior, in the process of living in and with the work I found that it had its own shape and architecture, in a way that felt more witnessed by me than written. Ultimately, I wrote the book for myself. It's not popular to say such a thing – more admirable, perhaps, to say that one has written for a specific person or group of people; for a son or a daughter or a parent. But to write this book for any other purpose would ultimately defeat the objective of its very subject manner – the not unpolitical idea that there is a world outside of the self, and a world inside the self, and that this often far more strange, queer and untethered interior landscape can, if fertilised by the rigour of our attention, offer untold gifts for how we might live and move through our collective world in this fraught time with greater possibility and freedom.

VICTORIA RECOMMENDS

M. NourbeSe Philip, *She Tries Her Tongue, Her Silence Softly Breaks* (Wesleyan University Press); Jay Bernard, *Surge* (Chatto); Layli Long Soldier, *Whereas* (Graywolf); Emily Berry, *Stranger, Baby* (Faber); Aracelis Girmay, *The Black Maria* (BOA Editions); Lucille Clifton, *The Collected Poems of Lucille Clifton* (1965-2010) (American Poets Continuum); Raymond Antrobus, *The Perseverance* (Penned in the Margins); Linda Gregg, *All of it Singing* (Graywolf).

NOT QUIET AS IN QUIET BUT

as in peaceful /
as in slow to anger /
as in shy /
as in sulking or sullen /
as in nice /
as in clean, tree-lined streets /
as in well-resourced libraries /
as in good, outstanding schools /
as in not much new /
as in no news is good news /
as in the war is over; has been for decades now /
as in early to bed / curled up with a book /
as in the newborn is sleeping /
as in TV barely audible /
as in subtitles /
as in subtext /
as in someone should've done something /
as in don't just do something, stand there /
as in could & should but wouldn't /
as in well the British are / so polite /
as in placid /
as in placated /
as in nuanced / complicated /
as in careful it's a conflict, not a siege, a conflict /
as in objective /
as in both sides /
as in well behaved /
as in safe /
as in too quiet /
as in almost silent /
as in almost no sirens /

I VICTORIA ADUKWEI BULLEY

LOST BELONGING

I
left
my bag
on the train
under the table.
Forgot it, looking
at the sun as I rolled
home into the city. Gold
was spilling from the frame
of a skyscraper & it looked
like a fire but it was only nature
reflecting off of steel. It was nature,
at it again, refracting from the metals
of this skin that we have grown so lately.
Everything is going to break & I must get
home before it does, or doesn't yet, or buckles.
Back to the locked shut door, to the batteries +/−
all dashed from the clock, & the blinds closed tight,
a millipede of stinging eyes, red light crashing through
from the place behind them.   *Mother,*   *where else can I go?*

VICTORIA ADUKWEI BULLEY

SYLVIA LEGRIS

Sylvia Legris is a critically acclaimed Canadian poet whose "work crackles with exuberant wackiness" (CBC/Radio-Canada). She was born in Winnipeg, Manitoba, and is the author of the poetry collections *The Hideous Hidden*, *Pneumatic Antiphonal*, and *Nerve Squall* (winner of the Griffin Poetry Prize and Pat Lowther Award). Legris lives in Saskatoon, Saskatchewan.

GARDEN PHYSIC

GRANTA | £10.99 | PBS PRICE £8.25

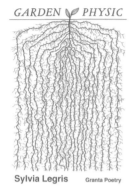

GARDEN 🌱 PHYSIC

Sylvia Legris   Granta Poetry

As the title proposes, the latest offering from Canadian poet Sylvia Legris presents us with a rich botanical panorama. The collection, her fifth, is packed with all the natural and vivid imagery you'd typically find in a garden – nettle, blossom, ferns and of course, roses. Yet Legris has a remarkable skill to turn the traditional landscape poem (which risks cliché) into a complex schema of phytology, thought and communication.

> At the center of the garden the heart.
> *Red as any rose.* Pulsing
> balloon vine. Love in a puff.
> Heartseed, heart-of-the-earth.
> A continuous flow of red.

Garden Physic is an immense panegyric, a testament to the power of environmentally minded poetry that concerns itself with the relationship between humans and the natural world. Gardens have often been thought of as sanctums and so at the core of the book's project is the overwhelming bid towards healing. A reparative yearning moves the poems into a place of restoration, rejuvenation, and new beginnings.

Neologisms pepper the text as we discover in 'Violet':

> April opens the musty secundina.
> Equinox the half-melt rot.
> Easter the thin asquintable light.

Legris' experimental approach adds another layer to the uncertainties of the garden. Syntax is compounded, names of flora are formalised then poeticised with an encyclopaedic grasp of taxonomies. The plants take on human personalities, objects are renamed, replaced, destroyed, and preserved. In Legris' garden the wild is not seeking out the human hand, but rather the human sings in praise of the wild and its magic.

Illustrations by the author of various plants are interspersed throughout the four sections of the book, which when merged with such eclectic diction, provide a humour, a child-like love, wonder and reverence for the world of gardens.

ANTHONY ANAXAGOROU

SYLVIA LEGRIS

Each collection of poetry I've written has led organically to the next one. The seeds for *Garden Physic* were planted during the writing of *The Hideous Hidden* (2016), which included poems that teased out the linguistic intersections of botany and glands. I made my first timid, though determined, attempts at gardening in 2013. Before writing a poem, there is mulling and digging, making a mess. The same is true for planting. In poetry as in gardening, much of the work is in preparing the ground. "In god's name the rototilling! The limb-sized roots," says my version of Pedanius Dioscorides, exasperated by his backyard garden. In preparing my own run-ragged backyard plot, I used only a fork, a hoe, and my hands. The roots that remained from a long-gone blue spruce were limb-sized, pulpy, and decaying. My hands digging into the earth felt as if they were digging into a profound intuitive anatomy. I felt like a surgeon when I attacked the ligament-like tangles of volunteer elm roots.

As with my previous poetry, what first and foremost drives *Garden Physic* is language. The more I worked in the soil, the more I became fascinated by and obsessed with the language associated with plants and horticulture, with the history and complexity of this language. How thrilled I was to discover the many plants named after parts of the human body: Five Fingers Grass, Heart Trefoil, Lungwort, Skeletonweed... Could one grow an anatomically arranged garden? It was in pondering this question that I envisioned what would become a core poem of the collection, 'The Garden Body: A Florilegium.' Once this poem flourished into its final form, I could imagine the full scope and shape of *Garden Physic*. This collection, to me, feels like a conversation, or maybe a series of conversations, a perennial garden party of multifarious voices and plants, "plants of antiquity and plants impending."

SYLVIA RECOMMENDS

The following titles are among those that have captured my attention during the most recent, perhaps weirdest seasons of the pandemic: Maria Stepanova, *War of the Beasts and the Animals* (Bloodaxe); Dante Micheaux, *Circus* (Indolent Books); Will Alexander, *The Combustion Cycle* (Roof Books) and *Refractive Africa* (Granta); Miroslav Holub, *Poems Before & After* (Bloodaxe); Elizabeth T. Gray, *Salient* (New Directions); Mei-mei Berssenbrugge, *A Treatise on Stars* (New Directions); Daisy Lafarge, *Life without Air* (Granta); G.C. Waldrep, *The Earliest Witnesses* (Carcanet).

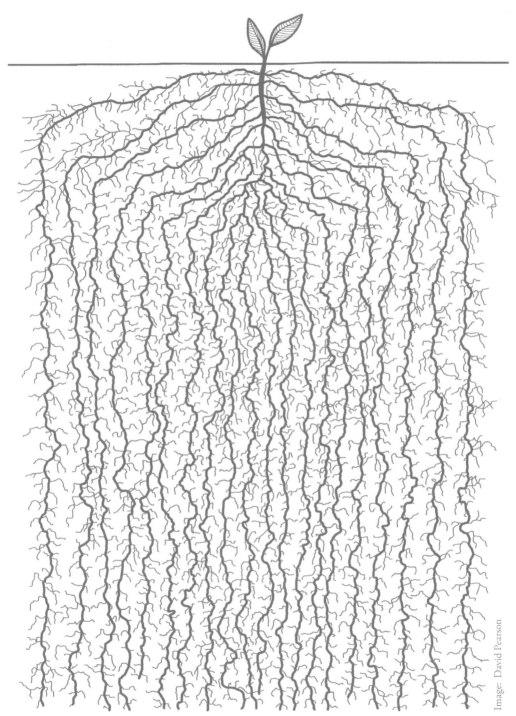

This first poem about the last book is where the garden begins

PICK ME

Pours it on thick as theriac the bush-
whacking physicians' treacly heal-alls.
The calls to arm thyself then the *Hail!*
Hail! pronouncements, the decrees.

The tinctures of vitriol, of Jesuit's bark.
The rough cathartics, the hell-
storming mercury. The bougies and fumes,
the fumigations, the fomentations.

Then equal parts bake-house and bagnio.
The poison-fed. The fever-starved. The
come-one-come-all the peccant-sweated.

DENISE SAUL

Denise is the author of two pamphlets, *White Narcissi* (Flipped Eye Publishing) and *House of Blue* (Rack Press) which were both Poetry Book Society Pamphlet Choices. She is the recipient of the Geoffrey Dearmer Prize (2011) and a Fellow of The Complete Works. Denise holds a PhD in Creative Writing (poetry) from the University of Roehampton. She won an Arts Council England's Grant for the Arts Award, for the delivery of her video poem collaborative project, *Silent Room: A Journey of Language*. This project can be found at www.silent-room.net.

THE ROOM BETWEEN US

PAVILION POETRY | £9.99 | PBS PRICE £7.50

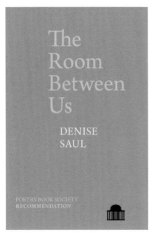

When Denise Saul's mother was diagnosed with aphasia, a condition which affects speech and communication, her role from daughter to carer inspired much of her debut collection *The Room Between Us*. The book explores the ways families go on interacting with each other when language fails, collapses or is rendered insufficient. The opening title-poem probes into both privacy and agency, through the function of rooms in a house:

> I give up trying to lift you from the floor
> as the room is no longer between us.

We see boundaries blur with little to cordon off sections. The mind, with its responsibility to care for a mother, becomes the only way to demarcate space, and so it's here where language is needed to connect/disconnect those varying aspects.

As the collection develops, we become aware of how bodily agency, a looming sense of frustration and hope, all work together to complicate individualism. Yet the carer in Saul's world is also committed and selfless while living a life restricted and emotionally demanding. Windows, a common noun which characterise much of the book's preoccupation with the inside and outside, invoke this duality, as shown in 'The White Room':

> There is a moment for meditation when the doctor leads me
> into the room with table, bed and cupboard. When he leaves, I
> look out of the small window. There's a view of other windows
> unknown.

At the centre of Saul's thinking is a constant reckoning with power. When language is fragmented and an individual must/wants to carry out familial duties, what is relinquished and what remains of a former life?

> I want to tell my mother about how she still holds light,
> and that this is the last day of seeing each other.

It's within this liminal space that poetry announces itself.

ANTHONY ANAXAGOROU

DENISE SAUL

Some of the poems in *The Room Between Us* can be considered as collaborative work. I recorded my mother's experience of the speech disability, aphasia, in my notebooks and afterwards read aloud my observations to her. Roman Jakobson's 1956 essay, "Two Aspects of Language and Two Types of Aphasic Disturbances" was a point of reference for my collection when I started to examine the relationship between brain trauma and speech.

I was mindful of my mother's presence or voice in *The Room Between Us*. She gave her consent to the publication of any forthcoming poems about her experiences of post stroke trauma. At first, observations of aphasic disturbances appeared slowly as I tried to recuperate most of my mother's aphasic voice and bodily experience.

For instance, the space inside the prose poem, 'Clopidogrel', is driven by the personal and the space outside this unit resists any form of closure.

> I was talking about the doctor or you were. I can't recall who
> spoke first even though I said clopidogrel and you said cabbage.

Silence is part of the caregiving experience. The gaps or spaces between lines, horizontally and vertically, are used to build boundaries between body and language. Some poems in the collection follow other experiences of loss: the death of a parent and sibling. In *The Room Between Us*, what is said and unsaid also invokes a close connection with nature and sound.

DENISE RECOMMENDS

Lyn Hejinian, *My Life* (Green Integer); Philip Gross, *Deep Field* (Bloodaxe); Jason Allen-Paisant, *Thinking with Trees* (Carcanet); Kayo Chingonyi, *A Blood Condition* (Chatto); Bhanu Kapil, *How To Wash A Heart* (Pavilion Poetry); Derek Walcott, *White Egrets* (Faber); Karen McCarthy Woolf, *Seasonal Disturbances* (Carcanet); Rushika Wick, *Afterlife As Trash* (Verve); Cath Drake, *The Shaking City* (Seren); Dawn McGuire, *The Aphasia Café* (IFSF publishing).

STONE ALTAR

I am not sure how the stone travelled
from British Guiana but the story goes
my mother brought it to England to remind her
of a passing like the way one remembers
the flight of a bird by keeping its feather.
What I thought was limestone was chalk
passed down from grandmother Frances
found among other stones in a black handbag
pushed to the back of a cabinet.
That autumn I asked my sister to tell me about
the stone when I sifted through the possessions.
When chalk gave away some dust, she held it
up to the light and told me about
other things in a world of decay.
It seemed easy enough for her to
wipe away the dust from her fingers.
No-one receives what they truly want.
It took me a while to understand all of this
when I placed the chalk on an altar
next to blue kyanite stones I collected.

THE ROOM BETWEEN US

There you are, beside the telephone stand,
waiting for me in a darkened room
when I force open the white door.
There you lie, behind it.

I never found out why you grabbed
a pewter angel instead of the receiver
when you tried to call me that morning.
I give up trying to lift you from the floor

as the room is no longer between us.
You point again to the Bible, door, wall
before I whisper, *It's alright, alright,*
now tell me what happened before the fall.

Image: Tom Hines

OCEAN VUONG

Ocean Vuong is the author of the critically acclaimed poetry collection *Night Sky with Exit Wounds* and the *New York Times* bestselling novel *On Earth We're Briefly Gorgeous*. A recipient of the 2019 MacArthur "Genius" Grant, he is also the winner of the Whiting Award and the T.S. Eliot Prize. His writings have been featured in *The Atlantic*, *Harper's Magazine*, *The Nation*, *The New Republic*, *The New Yorker* and *The New York Times*. Born in Saigon, Vietnam, he currently lives in Northampton, Massachusetts.

RECOMMENDATION

TIME IS A MOTHER

CAPE | £14.99 | PBS PRICE £11.25

"This is the best day ever / I haven't killed a thing since 2006" begins the highly anticipated *Time Is A Mother* from poet and novelist Ocean Vuong. Readers can expect to find more of Vuong's captivating verse, a high-lyric poet who seamlessly merges the personal with the political, the sentimental with the profane. The idea of the family, the son and friend play perhaps a more central role in this collection when compared to his 2016 debut *Night Sky With Exit Wounds*.

These are poems very much invested in care and renewal, in violence and its counterpart – protection. Throughout we notice an ongoing inquiry into what time does to human relations; how it manages to establish intimacy and longing, desire and need. The poems offer a confessional space enabling us to become part of another's private world. The epistolary poem 'Dear Peter' works around this landscape of disclosure:

> they treat me well
> here they don't
>   make me forget
> the world like you
>   promised but oh well
> I'm back inside
>   my head
> where it's safe
>   cause I'm not
> there the Xanax
>   dissolves...

Time becomes a recurring motif – poems address people no longer here or who appear to be unreachable in some capacity. While much of the book feels personal and specific Vuong manages to hold the reader with a poetry that is at once universal and porous. Lines remain highly quotable with an undertone of threat, redemption and tenderness. This is a collection fixated on the ways distance and longing play out, how they transmute and transgress into a wider plane. In the final poem 'Woodworking at the End of the World' the speaker announces:

> In a field, after everything, a streetlamp,
> shining on a patch of grass.
> Having just come to life, I lay down under its warmth,
> & waited for a way.

| SELECTOR'S COMMENT

ANTHONY ANAXAGOROU

THE BULL

He stood alone in the backyard, so dark
the night purpled around him.
I had no choice. I opened the door
& stepped out. Wind
in the branches. He watched me with kerosene
– blue eyes. *What do you want?* I asked, forgetting I had
no language. He kept breathing,
to stay alive. I was a boy –
which meant I was a murderer
of my childhood. & like all murderers, my god
was stillness. My god, he was still
there. Like something prayed for
by a man with no mouth. The green-blue lamp
swirled in its socket. I didn't
want him. I didn't want him to
be beautiful – but needing beauty
to be more than hurt gentle
enough to hold, I
reached for him. I reached – not the bull –
but the depths. Not an answer but
an entrance the shape of
an animal. Like me.

NOT EVEN (AN EXTRACT)

Long ago, in another life, on an Amtrak through Iowa, I saw, for a few blurred seconds, a man standing in the middle of a field of winter grass, hands at his sides, back to me, all of him stopped there save for his hair scraped by low wind.

When the countryside resumed its wash of gray wheat, tractors, gutted barns, black sycamores in herdless pastures, I started to cry. I put my copy of Didion's *The White Album* down and folded a new dark around my head.

The woman beside me stroked my back, saying, in a midwestern accent that wobbled with tenderness, *Go on son. You get that out now. No shame in breakin' open. You get that out and I'll fetch us some tea.* Which made me lose it even more.

She came back with Lipton in paper cups, her eyes nowhere blue and there. She was silent all the way to Missoula, where she got off and said, patting my knee, *God is good. God is good.*

I can say it was gorgeous now, my harm, because it belonged to no one else.

To be a dam for damage. My shittyness will not enter the world, I thought, and quickly became my own hero.

Do you know how many hours I've wasted watching straight boys play video games?

Enough.

Time is a mother.

Lest we forget, a morgue is also a community center.

In my language, the one I recall now only by closing my eyes, the word for *love* is *Yêu*.

And the word for *weakness* is *Yêu*

How you say what you mean changes what you say.

Some call this prayer, I call it watch your mouth.

Rose, I whispered as they zipped my mother in her body bag, *get out of there.*

Your plants are dying.

Enough is enough.

Time is a motherfucker, I said to the gravestones, alive, absurd.

Body, doorway that you are, be more than what I'll pass through. Stillness. That's what it was.

The man in the field in the red sweater, he was so still he became, somehow, more true, like a knife wound in a landscape painting.

Like him, I caved.

I caved and decided it will be joy from now on. Then everything opened. The lights blazed around me into a white weather

and I was lifted, wet and bloody, out of my mother, into the world, screaming

and enough.

HOLLY HOPKINS

Holly Hopkins grew up in Berkshire and London and now lives in Manchester. Her debut pamphlet *Soon Every House Will Have One* won the Poetry Business Pamphlet Competition and was the Poetry Book Society Pamphlet Choice. Holly has been an assistant editor of *The Rialto*. She received an Eric Gregory Award and a Hawthornden Fellowship and was shortlisted for the inaugural Women Poets' Prize. Her poems featured in *Carcanet New Poetries VIII* and have been published in *The Guardian, The Telegraph* and *TLS*.

THE ENGLISH SUMMER

PENNED IN THE MARGINS | £9.99 | PBS PRICE £7.50

The English Summer is the long-awaited debut collection from Holly Hopkins. But unlike the damp squib of a wet July, nothing in this honed, humane, and brilliantly inventive volume disappoints. As the title poem implies, this is not a poet inclined towards state-of-the-nation grandstanding, but one who levels a gaze altogether more wry, and incisive:

> Dun-coloured endangered species of specialist interest;
> best found on grungy paths, behind gabardines,
> near shoes on school radiators...

What starts as a humorous field guide to this raincoated species (the English in summer) begins to admit, by its second stanza, a more sinister vision: the sun's unaccustomed glare evokes the "fearsome firestorm" of climate change and "agricide", the ecological metaphor of "invasive species". In other words, despite the gentle self-mockery of its premise, nothing is safe or staid in a poem like this.

One of the delights of this book is Hopkins's imagination, which unspools in a series of magical what ifs, where the poet tweaks a small premise in the universe to reveal something unexpected: zombies that turn out not to be "flesh-robots" but "excellent listeners", or country churches that "slip their moorings in the night / and glide down tarmac roads / to a city where evangelicals / are taking over bingo halls". Hopkins's inventiveness is no less on show in her extraordinary facility for metaphor, reminiscent of the best moments in Craig Raine – or rather, perhaps, the way that Martianism honed the eye of a poet like Hannah Sullivan. For Hopkins, the best metaphors startle:

> a lead-lined coffin is better than Tupperware
> and the child's face was perfect as a new bar of soap.

Or watch this breathtaking leap, as a parcel containing a smashed vase is posted through a letterbox:

> the wreckage
> sliding like tectonic plates.

> This is how we are born,
> our skulls knit in our teens.
> The grotesque movement enables safe delivery.

SARAH HOWE

THE ENGLISH SUMMER

Dun-coloured endangered species of specialist interest;
best found on grungy paths, behind gabardines,
near shoes on school radiators, wet socks at work.
A furred creature, hood-hidden, brolly-blinded, shy.

The invasive species: a fearsome firestorm
of peeled blue sky. Allelopathic leaf-crisper,
river-fading grass-bleacher, ice-cream smiling
skin-killer, furze-burning-forest-eater, agricide.

See the burn-blisters on the ridge of this ear.
See water rationing. See heat oedema. See dizziness.

CLAIRE TRÉVIEN

Claire Trévien is the Breton-British author of several books including *The Shipwrecked House* which was longlisted for the *Guardian* First Book Awards. She founded Sabotage Reviews and its Saboteur Awards to support independent literature, running them both until 2018. She now lives in her native Brittany, France, with her two cats and copious painting supplies.

Marie Lando has been writing stories, poems and lyrics since a very young age and started making music five years ago under the stage name grabyourface. Well versed in creating intense and dark sonic atmospheres, translating Claire's book was a familiar and enjoyable experience. After years of living in Ireland and England and gaining experience in video game translation, they now live in the south of France with many animals.

TRANSLATION CHOICE

OUR LADY OF TYRES
TRANSLATED BY MARIE LANDO
BROKEN SLEEP BOOKS | £8.99 | PBS PRICE £6.75

Our lady of tyres
Notre dame des pneus
Claire Trévien
Translation: Marie Lando

POETRY BOOK SOCIETY TRANSLATION CHOICE

Broken Sleep Books

This is a book of protest, but not in the sense that it speaks urgently or bears witness to contemporary suffering. Rather, Trévien takes as a point of departure the militant and successful protest of the women of Plogoff in Brittany against a proposed nuclear power plant. Beginning with their voices and actions – "a quiet crowd with a microphone and a fire" who "will set fire to your yes / until it crumbles away", the book spirals out through wider themes of belonging and resistance in the poets' own life, threaded throughout with reflection on the role of poetry itself.

> ...I open my mouth,
> and only stones come out

The poet mourns, but at the same time, "they say nothing hurts more than a tongue." What is the point of writing, when it cannot capture the thick and smelly reality of a sheep? ("Literal sheep. Not poetry sheep.") And what are the dangers of the poetry of commemoration, if "when the historians came / our skin was no longer our skin"? There are no more answers in this book than any other, except for the necessity of the writing itself until the writing is done.

Our Lady of Tyres is an unusual Translation Choice, in that it was written in English and then translated into French, published as a bilingual first edition. I wish this striking choice were a good deal more common for English language poets. English is here no longer posing as a universal language of literary access, but something contingent and pliable. Marie Lando's French is as clear and sharp as Trévien's English, the two languages working together for a more complex whole. The verse itself reflects on this necessary uncertainty:

> lucky to live between two languages
> never needing to get too comfortable with either.

Poet and translator complement each other:

> leurs
> langues s'épanouissant et déclinant à la lumière.

SELECTOR'S COMMENT

HARRY JOSEPHINE GILES

THAT IS THE WAY I WANTED TO BEGIN

with your voices crowding
at my teeth, choking their path
to the front. Does a story
stop being a story when it reaches you?
There's a Marie-Paule and a Fanch
and a Thérèse, and a bundle of others
with the hoods of their green or yellow
coats slick with the rain, a slingshot
slung around their necks. The rivers
and the women carry stones in their pockets.
They have faces I know but don't know,
the features so familiar I could create a composite
without looking. I open my mouth,
and only stones come out.

avec vos voix s'amassant contre
mes dents, s'étranglant vers l'avant.
Est-ce qu'une histoire arrête d'en être une
lorsque tu l'entends?
Il y a une Marie-Paule,
un Fanch, une Thérèse et une foule d'autres
avec les capuches de leurs manteaux verts
ou jaunes ruisselant de pluie, un lance-pierre
lacé autour du cou. Les rivières
et les femmes portent des cailloux dans leurs poches.
Elles ont des visages connus mais inconnus,
leur physionomie tellement familière
que je pourrais créer un composite sans les regarder.
J'ouvre ma bouche et seules des pierres en sortent.

HELEN BOWELL

Helen Bowell is a poet and producer based in London. She is a co-director of Dead [Women] Poets Society, an Arts Council England-funded collective which seeks to "resurrect" women poets of the past through events and online. She co-guest-edited the *Modern Poetry in Translation* focus on dead women poets in Autumn 2020. Helen is a Ledbury Poetry Critic and a graduate of The Writing Squad, the London Library Emerging Writers Programme, London Writers Awards and the Roundhouse Poetry Collective. In 2020, she won the Bronze Creative Future Writers' Award and was commended in the Mslexia Poetry Competition. She was Poetry Business's first digital Poet in Residence in February 2021. Her poems have appeared in *Magma, Under the Radar, 100 Poems To Save The Earth* (Seren, 2021), *The Book of Bad Betties* (Bad Betty Press, 2021) and elsewhere. She works at The Poetry Society.

THE BARMAN
BAD BETTY PRESS | £6.00 |

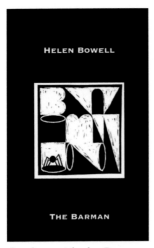

HELEN BOWELL

THE BARMAN

I found myself returning again and again to *The Barman* by Helen Bowell, drawn in by its humour and bittersweet heartache. Over the course of this surreal, occasionally romantic relationship between the speaker and an anonymous Barman, cracks begin to open up beneath the surface. Something dark and uncertain threatens to spill over the edges of the poem:

and I think about the knife-sharpener in the top drawer
and I think about how I want my life to be
and answering Bradley Walsh's question
about Edvard Munch, *The Scream*,
I say out loud, *The Scream*.

The speaker converses with herself as much as she does with the Barman, who doesn't quite see her the way she sees herself. Many poems explore these gaps in intimacy, this space between what we say and what we mean, between being seen and being invisible. One poem, 'Monsieur le Barman', negotiates the complexity of her mixed and multilingual heritage:

Ma grand-mère ne savait parler que cantonais.

佢歸西.

I want to say all this to the barman, but I think it would be too much.

All these silences begin to spill over. All these feelings become "too much"; they cannot be contained. With tenderness and an uncanny directness, *The Barman* seems to capture how it feels to be alive here and now, as we go about our days "not letting the news in", "signing petitions between gulps of tea". The poems are spacious enough to hold this unnamed strangeness, these slippages and gaps, heartbreaks large and small. And the character of the Barman is an excellent contemporary conceit devised by the poet to interrogate otherness from a vantage point that gives us a three-dimensional point of reference and access. 'Back Story' stands out as a poem of childhood. It leaves us with another slightly absurd scene, this time triumphant:

and I beat my wings
till the white vans and boys
in their bad uniforms
blew out out out to sea

BARMAN IN EDEN

In the autumn, the barman and I visit Eden.
They have put up signs since the last time I was here.

Some say DO NOT WALK ON THE GRASS;
others inform guests about the mass extinction.

A dragonfly bumps into a leaf. A peregrine
falcon nose-dives. A mother asks us for money.

I want to change everything
and nothing. The barman takes my hand,

suggests a tea break. I buy a fresh scone,
the exact shape of the barman's fist.

In the gift shop, we touch everything:
HOPE is printed in big letters on tea towels.

I know time is measured in Celsius.
At least I have enjoyed the seasons.

When we go home, even the sun
looks away.

SUMMER BOOK REVIEWS

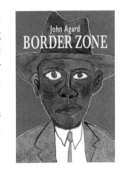

Well into the fifth decade of his poetry career, John Agard's *Border Zone* shows little sign of the elder statesman slowing down. His breezy lyrics and polysyllabic rhymes keep the long sequences that bookend the collection afloat. His flair for persona allows the book some of its more incisive political analysis and imaginative recontextualising of British (literary) history. Celebratory even in its moving elegies for friends and heroes, *Border Zone* is a work of joy from an old master.

APRIL | BLOODAXE | £12.00 | PBS PRICE £9.00

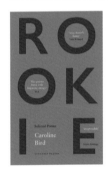

Caroline Bird's selected poems are both surreal and playful. These narrative poems deal with the precarious nature of life with wit and humour. Lines like "planting daffodils in a bucket of milk" shock in their beauty, and the poem 'Checkout', "An angel / approaches with a feedback form asking / how I'd rate my life", has a similar effect. Bird's poems are a testament to the limitless possibility of how language can transform, uplift, and help us make sense of the world.

MAY | CARCANET | £12.99 | PBS PRICE £9.75

Kayo Chingonyi's long awaited anthology calls attention to the "clear divisions in the poetry ecosystem across boundaries of race, class, and... gender". These poems make a space for subjectivity and resistance: a battle cry for urgent change, to challenge the pervasive whiteness of the British poetic establishment. Informed by community, communality, and persistence in the face of "overwhelming pressure", *More Fiya* is a vital experiment in grace; grief and rage; love and survival.

MAY | CANONGATE | £16.99 | PBS PRICE £12.75

I SUMMER READING

LEDBURY CRITICS TAKEOVER

These deeply personal poems are rich with the lexicon of Gypsy, Roma and Traveller life. They bear the weight of suspicion and violence directed towards those who live within the rhythms and currents of the natural world. Laden with verbs that sing, these are not poems of introspection: they are as utilitarian and active on the page as those who "skim... and can't settle" on our landscape. Many of the poems hold notes of such tenderness, they stop your breath.

MAY | BLOODAXE | £10.99 | PBS PRICE £8.25

P.J. HARVEY: ORLAM
REVIEWED BY LEAH JUN OH

P.J. Harvey rises again to the mantle of bard to lend her lyricism to a cyclical, seasonal collection that riddles and rhymes. Gruesomely unnerving and full of curses, *Orlam* follows young Ira, equally bewitched by the "foul freedom" of the woodlands, as by her ghostly girlhood idol –"Wyman-Elvis". Harvey proudly draws upon the Dorset dialect to write a collection that knows where it comes from – and knows the chilling nature of its lot in life.

APRIL | PICADOR | £16.99 | PBS PRICE £12.75

FOOTPRINTS: AN ANTHOLOGY OF NEW ECOPOETRY
REVIEWED BY MAGGIE WONG

Charlie Baylis and Aaron Kent have gathered wide-ranging environmental writing from over ninety poets. Instead of retracing the "far too easy" path of "say(ing) climate change is bad", these poems approach the climate crisis through innovative new lenses, with striking found text and list poems. The many emerging voices featured in *Footprints* offer vital hope and provocation in an age when "creativity is all we've got left" a haunting reminder about what it means to be human.

JUNE | BROKEN SLEEP | £11.99 | PBS PRICE £9.00

BOOK REVIEWS

ANDRÉ NAFFIS-SAHELY: HIGH DESERT
REVIEWED BY MAGGIE WONG

André Naffis-Sahely's compelling and deeply researched second collection begins in California but blossoms into a globally engaged meditation on history, migration, inclusion, and justice. Drawing on found text from diaries to academic manuscripts and traversing across North America, Europe, and Asia, *High Desert* is at once humble and unafraid. "You cannot rescue history from dust – / all you save one day will crumble / in your hand", Naffis-Sahely writes in a haunting reminder about what it means to be human.

JUNE | BLOODAXE | £10.99 | PBS PRICE £8.25

ANITA PATI: HIDING TO NOTHING
REVIEWED BY SHASH TREVETT

Anita Pati's debut collection utilises form and language to devastating effect. The central section is an elegy for all the "neverborns" and the women who were mothers all too briefly. In other poems, uncompromising in scope and content, women's bodies take centre stage: are shown as being overly scrutinised, found lacking, raped or put under the knife. Channelling a myriad of voices, Pati speaks commandingly for those who, though suffering, continue to see "only stars".

APRIL | PAVILION | £9.99 | PBS PRICE £7.50

PHOEBE POWER: BOOK OF DAYS
REVIEWED BY DAVE COATES

Phoebe Power's *Book of Days* concerns a month on the 500-mile Camino de Santiago, populated by vacationing professionals, vegan menus, and yoga instructors. The book's narrative is comprehensive and the cast of fellow travellers sprawling, but *Book of Days* seems reluctant to reflect on what it witnesses. Its final word, that pilgrimage is a state of the soul and not a fixed time and place, is convincing, but leaves the book's journey feeling hollow. What did it all mean?

APRIL | CARCANET | £11.99 | PBS PRICE £9.00

SUMANA ROY: V.I.P. VERY IMPORTANT PLANT
REVIEWED BY SHALINI SENGUPTA

V.I.P. opens with a nod to Jagadish Chandra Bose: a polymath, physicist, biologist, and botanist whose work on plant physiology feeds Sumana Roy's thinking. This collection continues Roy's trailblazing new work on plant humanities: one that is prompted by the desire to reposition ecocritical literature and render it more open to the experiences of the marginalised other. In these quietly subversive lines, expectations are undone: of ecologies, plants, people. Roy has produced a revelation and a reckoning.

APRIL | SHEARSMAN | £10.95 | PBS PRICE £8.22

SAPPHO: SONGS AND POEMS: TRANS. CHRIS PREDDLE
REVIEWED BY LEAH JUN OH

Chris Preddle's translation of Sappho is accessible and lyrically traditional. He pursues a "connected sense" of Sappho's fragments, avoiding, where possible, the gaps in the text. In light of this, Preddle acknowledges where he employs "scholarly conjectures" to maintain his flow. Heavily annotated, Preddle's exposition at times distracts from the poem in question. He is generous to let the reader in on the joke – but to do so, he has to explain it.

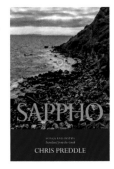

APRIL | THE IRISH PAGES | £14.00 | PBS PRICE £11.25

PAUL TRAN: ALL THE FLOWERS KNEELING
REVIEWED BY MEMOONA ZAHID

The linear progression from trauma to healing is complicated in *All the Flowers Kneeling*, where poems with lyric ambiguity ask the reader to see survival not as an end point, but as a journey, back and forth. The structure of Tran's debut collection evokes this temporality, the placement of poems like 'Scheherazade / Scheherazade' which start and end the collection pierce the membrane of a fixed notion of identity by creating a conversation with the self – "a poem is a mirror".

MAY | PENGUIN PRESS | £12.99 | PBS PRICE £9.75

BOOK REVIEWS

SUMMER PAMPHLETS

EVE ESFANDIARI-DENNEY: MY BODIES THIS MORNING THIS EVENING

My Bodies This Morning This Evening is both moving and playful, always attentive, caught between the surreal and the profoundly personal. Here are poems about the body's different states, womanhood, love, borders, and family. Esfandiari-Denney weaves a dense and vivid world where there is "a place to tread between hell and the light from the fridge" and "the reason the bird sings in the morning is to confirm she survived the night".

BAD   BETTY   PRESS | £6.00 |

ED. ELLA DUFFY: SEEDS & ROOTS

In this vital eco-anthology, Ella Duffy gathers "poems which make us alert to the true existence of seeds". Here, seeds tell stories of "culture and place, rebellion and resistance", belonging and uprooting. These are poems of "roar and bloom", bursting with life, finely attuned to the earth and the symbiotic relationship of plants and humans. From Vahni Capildeo to Major Jackson, each poem takes root and "renews (your) kinship with growing things".

HAZEL   PRESS | £10.00 |

REBECCA HURST: THE FOX'S WEDDING

Part of the Emma Press Art Squares series, this enchanting debut by Rebecca Hurst is beautifully illustrated by Reena Makwana. Opening with 'The Unreliable Narrator', these poems circle around mythical forests, "this wood has a thousand exits and entrances", where creatures flit in and out of focus. Hurst weaves together, and subtly unravels, "the memetics of fairy tales" from frog princes to gingerbread boys. Full of folklore and forested states of being, *The Fox's Wedding* is a beguiling feat of whimsy and wonder.

EMMA   PRESS | £10.00 |

NICOLA NATHAN: HEKATE

HEKATE
Nicola Nathan

Hekate is Nicola Nathan's debut pamphlet and an exploration of the Greek goddess of the underworld, oracles, crossroads and witchcraft. Here Hekate is both *androphonos* (eater of men) and *polyodynos* (full of pain). Each side of the goddess is a mirror for women to perceive themselves through, as well as a carefully listening confidante. "Hekate, Mother... / Days I feel / there's no more / to my name / than the flaunt / of blood / on a white bride sheet."

DARE   GALE   PRESS | £7.00 |

MAYA C. POPA: DEAR LIFE

Selected by Daljit Nagra and Pascale Petit as winner of the 2021 International Book & Pamphlet Competition, *Dear Life* is suffused with love and death, literature and legacy. In quiet, entrancing verse Popa explores the experience of living and the great questions which come with it, using the touchstones of poets who have come before, history, and the natural world. There is a mournful quality to *Dear Life*, but in equal parts it is tender, soothing, and restorative.

SMITH | DOORSTOP | £6.50 |

SAMUEL TONGUE: THE NAKEDNESS OF FATHERS

This eclectic sequence of vibrant, mesmeric poems oscillates between the metaphysical and the hyperreal. Samuel Tongue explores depictions of faith and culture through strange perspectives; the recurring image here is the museum, where artefacts divorced from their context are scrutinised like religious texts to divine their inner meanings. Here, the thematic potential of the supermarket and a journey through the streets of Google Earth are given meticulous care and attention. A rich, surprising, and rewarding pamphlet.

BROKEN   SLEEP   PRESS | £6.50 |

PAMPHLET REVIEWS

SUMMER BOOK LISTINGS